The Winds Of Time

By

Andrew Beattie

Copyright © 2024 Andrew Beattie

ISBN: 978-1-917129-23-7

All rights reserved. No part of this publication may be reproduced, stored in a retrieval system, or transmitted in any form, or by any means, electronic, mechanical, photocopying, recording or otherwise without the prior permission in writing of the copyright holder, nor be otherwise circulated in any form or binding or cover than in which it is published and without a similar

Contents

Under a Parisian Sky 3

The Old House 4

Memories 5

The Young Lady With The Long Green Coat 7

The German Girl 8

Gone Too Soon 9

The Liberation of Laughter 10

A Summer of Repentance 11

These Fleeting Moments 12

Geraldine 14

My Goddess Has Gone 15

The Winds of Time 16

Raes' Wood 17

Through The Indulgence of Illusion 19

A Spiritual Journey 20

Reading With Sensitivity 21

A Lonely Thought 22

A Seed of Happiness 23

There's Worse Things Than Being Alone 24

Loved and Lost 25

That Sunday 26

Admiration 27

The Beautiful Lady From Whitehead 28

A Sobering Thought 29

We Shared	30
The Redhead	31
A Sequence of Artistic Activity	32
Escapism	33
Aughris	34
Before the Fall	36
The Golden Lady	37
A Reservoir of Desire	38
You Lie Under Grass	39
The Liverpool Air	40
The Sleepy Seaside Town	41
A Letter Never Sent	42

Under a Spring Parisian Sky

We walked through the streets late at night
Under a spring Parisian sky
The cafes and restaurants filled with a soft calming tone
Faces relaxed and contented, sipping on wine, eating so slowly.

We were lost in the night
You clenched my hand ever so tight
A worried look fell from doleful eyes
I, on the other hand felt at home in this cosmopolitan city.

We sat on a dark green wooden bench
You lay your head upon my shoulder
Whilst shedding a tear or two
I watched with enthusiasm long into the night
My senses were alive and breathed in the differentness.

The Old House

My mind wanders back in time to the sweet memories of the old house
As I slowly pass this distinctive building
A place of refuge from harsh reality
When to doubt my own sanity.

The first virginal snowflakes fall from the still night sky
Already they gather and take a firm hold upon the stony ground
Remembering back in time when you used to stand at your front door and kindly invite me into your hypnotic world
With a genuine comfortable smile upon your pretty face.

Wishing you were standing there right now, even for just a moment
Inviting me once more into your daring, individual world
Innocent childlike charm filled the empty spaces
Your uniqueness was like a precious stone, sparkling for all to see.

My mind deep in thought
Tears trickle down a solemn face
The snow gathers momentum upon the stony ground
As it freshly crunches below my clumpy winter shoes.

Memories

The light has went out
Tears from Heaven fall softly
Trickling to an uncaring world below
Whilst replenishing the garden flowers.

Lingering silence, test the waters
Contemplating isolation in the foreseeable future
Nothing but grey skies
This damn climate, unbearable.

I miss the innocence of laughter
Dancing of joyful noise
The freedom of movement
Teetering on the brink of hopelessness.

Most of all I miss those alcoholic afternoons
The endless sexual fulfilment
Joined at the hip
Comfortable as one.

You have been gone a whole year now
It seems like only yesterday
Memories of sadness fill a troubled mind
What a pitiful sight.

You are not here to lie with me anymore
To hold, touch, caress and cherish
Ah, the laughter has long since gone
I still cannot stop my thoughts from racing.

Many a time we walked from the Michael Ferguson roundabout
Passing by the rocket shaped chapel
Crossing the railway tracks in Dunmurry
Finally resting under an ancient tree.

How you loved to wash away your worries
Under that reliable tree
The memories will never fade
For you are always with me my dear.

The Young Lady With The Long Green Coat

She walked out of Waterstones with elegance
The young lady with the long green coat
On a Wednesday in February, late afternoon
The air was still but pretty cold.

Inside I glance along the bookshelves
Still wondering why I haven't made it
Still wondering about the young lady with the long green coat
Who was solemn in look and unmoved.

She walked towards Castle Street
Normal pace not swift of foot
Her eyes kept looking straight ahead
A mere possible thought on her mind, if any.

Slender, graceful and attractive
Smallish in height with short fair hair
With eyes a light blue
Calm and serene.

The young lady with the long green coat.

The German Girl

I met you on a winter's morning at an airport in Berlin
You spoke in fluent English
With a soft, warm smile upon your face
How friendly you were.

We talked a lot more, it felt so right
You said originally your family came from Dresden
I said, 'how cruel to be carpet-bombed
Two wrongs never make a right'.

You sat next to me on the airplane to Dublin
You held my hand, I felt flustered
I looked deeply into your Germanic green eyes
The look of divine beauty fell upon me.

Your hand went into a carrier bag
And took out a fancy notebook
You tore a little page from it
Then wrote down your phone number, along with the code for Germany.

Gone Too Soon

She was an actress in the early days of the silent film era
A major star between 1911 and 1917
Her career was at its height when she died at age 29
From injuries sustained in an automobile accident.

Adopted at the age of three
A daredevil at heart
She was known as 'Fearless Flow'
For taking risks and performing many of her own stunts.

A luminous gifted actress
Florence was also sensitive and poetic
A vigorous advocate for peace during World War I
A gorgeous starlet, an ugly death.

'To know Florence La Badie is to love her'
Jean Darnell, actress.

The Liberation of Laughter

Through the bleakest of days, your attributes are both benevolent and beneficial
Warming the coldest of hearts, as you trudge over pure fluffy snow
The dreamiest of eyes I have ever seen
A mind far beyond the pale.

I watch you pass the dreary neighbourhood in which I am chained
Wishing you belonged solely to me
I gradually infiltrate your calm, logical demeanour
Through a relentless and obsessive infatuation.

The impoverishment of a generation can someday rest
To obliterate the deepest complexity
Bring forth an impregnable breath of fresh air
And dance with the liberation of laughter.

A Summer of Repentance

Grey house after grey house after grey house
Look at the rain dancing, a sheer delight
Through the faint summer breeze
The sky as dark as a winter's night.

We ponder deeply from early morning
Whilst holding onto inner belief
The core of soul does languish on a creaky bed
Searching for hope, searching for redemption.

Sweaty naked bodies writhing against each other
The moaning from intense pleasure from the lack of restraint
The ecstasy sent us to another dimension, far beyond this troublesome world
Floating delicately as nature intended.

The Bangor air tastes like so many others
Silky skin, heady scent and a warm body
Connected by lust, passion and opportunity
As her large blue eyes looked deep into mine.

Sipping tea after tea after tea
The visualisation of a sense of loss
Excessive laughter through the loneliness and pain
To ease a burden and lack of self-worth.

Liberation hangs awkwardly in the muggy and fragrant air
Even under the weight of sedation
The transportation of a philosophical mind
Deep in art, a lover of wisdom.

These Fleeting Moments

Waiting impatiently for you in the nestled surroundings of the waterworks
A long lingering grin has given rise to idealistic contentment
Feeling like an overexcited teenager, as I manically move around
Eventually I sit down on a bench which is near the corner gate.

The seagulls flap their wings frantically by the water's edge
Squealing with rage as they fight amongst themselves over loose scraps of bread
The general public being the guilty culprit, having showered them with numerous loaves
Seagulls seem to be the wicked scavengers of the air
Whereas the beautiful swans glide elegantly along the pond
Disconnected amid unconcerned oblivion.

At last, I can see you near the bottom gate
Arriving at the bench within a short space of time
A slight lost look hangs over your delicate face
Though still managing a benevolent smile.

Golden hair like fresh shredded corn
I see confused misfortune in twinkling brown eye
Gently stroking your sweet, scented cheek
Then I wrap a long arm around that shapely body
Before we part company, I kiss your cold soft hand.

These fleeting moments are so very short
Smiling and blushing awkwardly towards one another
Sadly, walking a separate path
To muse with anticipation
Goodbye for now, desirable young woman.

Geraldine

You looked so lost the night I met you
You had run away from home in Newcastle, County Down
Running from life, running from yourself
It really was a lost weekend.

You missed your mother so much
She had died the year before
Your mind was in turmoil
The heart was deeply troubled.

A raven-haired beauty
Originally from Cookstown in County Tyrone
A great artist
With a delicate soul.

I sometimes wonder about you
Do you still walk along the beach alone
Through the winter storms
Who knows Geraldine, only you.

My Goddess Has Gone

The reopening of old wounds
Too late for damage limitation
Precautions have been judged inadequate
For by nature soft-hearted.

Dancing delicately as a snowflake
Activates a vacuum in the heart
A sadness in the voice
Many more snowflakes dance delicately.

Facing stiff challenging winds
The imprints on the sand have faded
A rogue wave smashes into nearby rocks
Creating a pool of instability.

A web of deceit
Stuck in quicksand
Sinking so fast
My goddess has gone.

The fairy tale disturbed and strewn
Darkness stretches over smooth sea glass
Heavily bruised by deep hurt
My goddess has gone.

The Winds of Time

I swept my arm around your shoulder
As we drifted aimlessly into another world
Rich blue waters reflected a sea of tranquillity
The winds of time fell upon us.

Writing washes away from the soul, the dust of a humdrum existence
A smile that shone and lit up my inner workings
Now an emotional tear of sadness falls for all to see
Though the kindness you have shown will never cease.

How you nurtured a once hidden talent
The keeper of an innocent dream that now bleeds
I won't disturb the slumber of feelings that have died
Love your life, poor as it is.

A critical thinker was born in 1964
Raised in the city of Belfast
Where the gun, bullet and bomb held court
And the hatred smiled easily upon another victim.

Raes' Wood

Walking through the narrow path on a still October day
With my woman who has her dog in hand
The crisp cold air lingers around our bodies
With the sound of a soft whisper.

Tree after tree after tree
Each different from the last
Some slouch over the narrow path
While others stand tall and mighty.

Fallen branches lie scattered
Our path soft, damp and murky
Not a sinner in sight, except for us
To indulge in a little escapism, gentle and peaceful.

We are now in the heart of the wood
A light wind appears from nowhere
The leaves from the trees dance a delicate delight
A drizzle falls from greyish clouds.

I stand and stare at nature
Wildflowers languish in forgotten soil
The wind delivers the smell of raindrops onto the leaves
Which replenishes what was lost.

The Lough, dark and mysterious
We could feel the eeriness on our shoulders
With the waves gently lapping at our feet
I throw a flat stone and watch it skim, which creates many ripples
I watch them drift into the unknown.

We stand under a mighty tree
Seeking shelter under its vast branches
I hold you close, we share lips
Love often exposes a vulnerability
The scattering of heart to the four corners.

We gaze into each other's soul
The senses sharpened like never before
Two worlds become one, we feast
An earthquake erupts
We cling as one spiritual being with the same lasting thought.

Through The Indulgence of Illusion

I am dying to hide in a hearty bosom
Or in a delicious womb
I walked here for peace of mind
Though I am surrounded by bloody tourists.

Cameras snapping, photos of everything and anything
Oh, they mean no harm
My mood is selfish today
I simply want to gather my thoughts.

A sensitive soul wants to be perfectly understood
Walking through life, denied expression
Dogged determination with no regret
How the world loves to scoff.

I retreat back into my shell
Through the indulgence of illusion
It's all I know and what I do best
Where nothing can harm a gentleman.

Listening to the sleepy sound of a water fountain
Basking in the therapeutic glow
The light August wind blows on a thoughtful mind
As young children run with an innocent smile.

A Spiritual Journey

Thank you for breathing life into me
For being with me every step of the way
Guiding me through all of life's ills
And for giving hope and renewing my faith.

You pour gifts upon my soul
Taking me on a spiritual journey
If it wasn't for you, I would be nothing
Thank you for everything.

You drive away so much pain
I find perfect inner peace
You are with me every single moment
If it wasn't for you, I would be insane by now.

Thank you!

Reading With Sensitivity

Longing for smothering, delicious kisses
Yearning from a cold and lonely bed
Too simply hold a soft pure hand
Through winter's rough terrain.

Sweet smiles form easily, connected at the hip
Reading with sensitivity into each other's thoughts
Gathering momentum as we race on an isolated beach
We hide behind an ageing shipwreck
To quench a lustful thirst.

Climbing upon my back I give a helping hand
Wandering speechless through windswept sand.

A Lonely Thought

The Spanish air etched into a burning mind and skin
As beautiful señoritas pass by on golden sand
A sincere and elegant look upon every face
With tight slim figures and long athletic legs.

Young men indulge in youthful bravado
Churning through crystal clear water on speedboats
A sudden brief rush of wind blows around the beach
Parasols fly through the air and land in shallow water
Folks struggle as they chase after them
I burst with a boyish giggle, for I find it rather amusing.

A handful of men walk briskly along selling soft drinks and beer
I chose to buy a couple of beers and my friend likewise
Tasting like manna straight out of Heaven
For it really does quench a man's thirst.

I feel lonely when I watch couples who are content in each other's arms
Smiling with affection as they look deeply into each other's eyes
I watch them spread suncream on each other's bodies
I look a little lost and bewildered.

The sea shimmers in the afternoon sunlight
As children wrestle with the gentle waves
By now the beer enhances a creative mind
I leap into the Mediterranean to cool my limbs
And to soothe a lonely thought.

A Seed of Happiness

We walk along an empty beach
As darkness happily falls
No sound to be heard
The still night demands respect.

A simple gentle walk takes place
The eyes are filled with wonder
Loins eagerly anticipate affection
Though hesitant out of fear of rejection.

I touch your cold white neck
Then stroke a smooth soft cheek
Embracing with such tenderness
As I kiss those inviting lips.

The weakness of the flesh, a necessity
To satisfy an age-old thirst
We devour each other's flesh on cool, dry sand
Two lustful bodies performing as one.

We struggle over a mound of earth
Back to the belly of our domain
Both groins a face of contentment
A seed of happiness has been resurrected.

I'm fond of you, though not in love
Common ground so hard to find
They have closed minds, closed ears and closed intellects
Whereas I have endured my illness with great fortitude.

There's Worse Things Than Being Alone

'There's something wrong with you
You're not quite right in the head'
She repeatedly said.

'Why are you not like others
You just lie lifeless in your bed'
She repeatedly said.

'You can't communicate properly
You're simply braindead'
She repeatedly said.

Spitting words in my direction
You see red
So, I fled
'Hopeless!'
She repeatedly said.

'There's worse things than being alone'
I repeatedly said.

Loved and Lost

I have lost the woman of my ultimate dream
How she fitted into the grand scheme
A soapy naked body behind a glass of frost
I partly quote from Tennyson
'Tis better to have loved and lost'.

My best friend, soulmate and ardent lover
In church the nervous laughter we tried desperately to smother
Hand in hand we walked everywhere together
Through the unpolluted atmosphere with dignity and freedom
Gentle as a feather.

That Sunday

That Sunday you left in the early hours
Taxi arrived and off you went to work
All the clothes that hung were gone
You left a watch in the drawer in mother's old room
The one I bought you for Christmas.

No word, no trace, since that early morning in June
I wrote you a poignant letter
But to no avail
Nothing since that Sunday.

Admiration

Fine healthy agile bones
You have something I desire
A look of sincerity upon a shy face
Sets my dormant flesh on fire.

As you pass by, I feel so nervous
The heart pounding in the chest
Catching me feebly gawk with admiration
Until I actually pluck up the courage, I cannot rest.

The Beautiful Lady From Whitehead

I sat in my local bar
And watched you from afar
The beautiful lady from Whitehead.

Delicate as a little flower
We only spoke for roughly an hour
The beautiful lady from Whitehead.

My mind did flow
Your voice tender and low
The beautiful lady from Whitehead.

You had to go
I know, I know
The beautiful lady from Whitehead.

It was time for bed
She said, she said
The beautiful lady from Whitehead
The beautiful lady from Whitehead.

A Sobering Thought

I lost you a long time ago
A regret falls onto a weary world
The sky as black as a deep winter sleep
The sea roars, spitting out anger.

I pushed you away through a broken mind
Whilst the heart still longed for affection
The sun was splitting the trees
But the soul ached for more.

I let you fly, free as a bird
Not fully knowing the consequences
I lost you then and I would lose you again
A sobering thought.

We Shared

We shared magnificent dreams
A breeding ground for optimism
Smiling, but silent
Showing delicate compassion
Never crippling conversation.

When I pass over to the next life
Our souls will be embedded on a cloud
Floating high around the atmosphere without a care
Building bridges throughout the solar system.

I wish you could wear my shoes
Then you could feel my earthly pain
Blistering heat melts my belief
If only the sky could speak.

Being sober is frightfully boring
Through sterile tedious plane
I miss the twinkle in the eye
Now, in a lonely grave you lie.

The Redhead

The redhead wild and free
Dancing upon a Sligo beach
Through the fresh spring winds
Nothing can hold this one down.

A happy smile flows easily upon a pretty face
Makeup-free, it was never a necessity
A natural look of beauty adorns ageless skin
Sixty now, I bet you still look no more than forty.

Sometimes I think I should call her
Other times I think I should write her a letter
I wasn't brave enough yesterday
I'm not brave enough today
Possibly tomorrow?

Fair skin runs without restraint
Dangling with a wicked sense of humour
An anger that would put fear into any man
But you are unique and unequalled in the world.

A Sequence of Artistic Activity

I read my poems in a quiet manner
Naked as the day I was born
You have faith and belief in my art
Quite possibly more than I have.

I had you several times on the bedroom floor
How meaningful to feel wanted again
The nakedness entwined, hands caressing skin, lips gently nibbled
Sweaty sex mixed with tears of joy.

The curtains were drawn to hide any drop of suspicion
The moody sky eventually burst unleashing an almighty anger
How it eased a troubled mind
Creating a sequence of artistic activity.

Now I sit with cider in hand
The mind wandering in reflective silence
Surely, it's not wrong to seek affection.
For this pitiful life is far too short.

Dreams fall slowly from the pillow
Into the obscene, obscure unknown
The life in us is like the water in the river
I raise a glass to absent friends.

Solid ground I yearn
I search and search, though cannot find
The sound of confusion lingers in the atmosphere
Perhaps my expectations are far too great?

Escapism

Contemplating life without you is not an option
For you light up many a pitiful day
I enter yet again into another difficult situation
Your qualities stretch far beyond normal recognition.

Brown eyes shine with hypnotic slowness
I willingly go forth
Sublimeness can be found within escapism
A dance of delight through weary shadows.

Holding me close in your saintly arms
Always, always, always bearing gifts
Refreshment, comfort, sanity and sanctuary
Levitate to a mystical plane
Far beyond this shambolic world.

Aughris

Waves roll by your shore, so peacefully
At last, the first signs of spring were evident
Sunlight burst through the glorious heavens
The meditation of inner radiance that is beyond sorrow.

A quaint, quiet pier stands nearby
A derelict house observes from a hillside
Where wildflowers sway in the morning light, perhaps seeking affection?
The earth soft from the battering of the wild Atlantic Ocean.

Along a winding path we meet friendly contented faces
Each bubbling with childlike enthusiasm
Walking towards the water's edge, I hold my woman close
We smile with ease, through a happiness that cannot be measured.

Darkness now falls upon the water
Many stars shine in the mesmerising sky
Struggling to skim our flattest stones
Laughing with a sense of innocence.

A seventeenth century thatched roof pub stands facing us
Full of decent wisecrack characters
They share their laddish tall tales
I smile out of kindness while drinking my Guinness.

Outside I discover a disused well
I throw in a coin and make a solemn wish
The well has corroded over time, I fear my wish will also
For world peace is just a dream that drops ever so slowly.

Before the Fall

This is where we swam
And this is where we lay
Under the sky of Uncle Sam
Day after day.

The November light held out
For a few hours or more
We were deep in love without a doubt
Fortune knocks once at least at every man's door.

A smile, laugh and a dance, we had it all
To your final welcome, I draw near
Life was almost perfect before the fall
All lost through insecurities and a hideous fear.

The Golden Lady

I think about her every moment of every day
The golden lady adorned with a summer freshness
She is soft-spoken and has a calm and easy-going demeanour
She is also highly sensitive to other people's emotions.

Breasts full, favourable and inviting
Give both life and worldly pleasure
Attracted by an intense magnetic power
Even though you're gone, you still mean the world to me.

A Reservoir of Desire

Intoxicated by your lingering passionate kisses
Cherishing every moment I share with you on God's earth
Stimulating my affection to a high degree of sustained devotion
To catch my breath in admiration every time I look upon your adorable face.

A reservoir of desire escalates in the cells of my heart
Bringing unshakeable stability into my once complex world
The happiness runs through my mind like never before
We continuously smile at each other whilst wrapped together in boundless love.

Playfully tickling under fine smooth linen
Nibbling inquisitive ear
Staring into the depths of your soul
Lying naked through the first taste of spring.

You Lie Under Grass

Under grass
You lie under grass
I still think about the past
You lie under grass.

Under grass
You lie under grass
You smoked and drank too much
Twinned iniquities that held a crutch
You lie under grass.

Under grass
You lie under grass
How you loved to dance
I could not break the trance
You lie under grass.

Under grass
You lie under grass
Now is the time for us
Push me under a morning bus
You lie under grass.

Under grass
You lie under grass.

The Liverpool Air

I watch with admiration from across the room
Light brown, shoulder-length wavy hair
You lift the spirit through winter, February gloom
Heart pulsating in the Liverpool air.

Peering from behind a deep meaningful book
A confident smile, which can easily cope
My simple world, you fairly shook
Eyes that glisten with tenderness and hope.

Laughter fills the room, natural language from an excitable student
More than occasionally, you catch my inquisitive eye
I sit slightly awkward, innocent and prudent
You're absolutely beautiful, no word of a lie.

The Sleepy Seaside Town

We walked through the sleepy seaside town
On a cold winter's day
The strong winds penetrate our clothes
Which were wet from heavy rainfall.

We walked into a bar at the edge of the town
And sat next to a roaring fire
We both had a drink or two
While we dried our clothes from the glowing heat of the fire.

We held hands and spoke softly
Looking deep into each other's eyes
I said, 'I love you' and you said, 'I love you'
The exchange came as no surprise.

The natural deep moment of intimacy was not lost.

A Letter Never Sent

I wrote you a letter just a few weeks ago
It still lies upon my kitchen table
Weary of an emotional outpouring
Though you are really not that kind of person.

I do miss you, we had so many good times
Drinking wine on a Sunday afternoon
Treated to a lavish meal
Lazy days, cosy nights, comfy blankets and a warm lady
It was so sad the way our relationship ended.

My every aspiration you listened attentively
You never judged nor condemned, for you believed
We let the world slide on by
Oh, so many poignant memories.